£3.

FLY
CASTING

The author with his National and International trophies.

FLY
CASTING

TECHNIQUES FOR THE MODERN ANGLER

James Tomlinson

ADAM & CHARLES BLACK
LONDON

First published 1984
by A. & C. Black (Publishers) Ltd.
35 Bedford Row, London WC1R 4JH
© 1984 James Tomlinson

ISBN 0-7136-2403-5

Tomlinson, James, 19---
    Fly casting.
    1. Fly casting
    I. Title
    799.1'2   SH454.2
    ISBN 0-7136-2403-5

Printed by R. J. Acford, Chichester, Sussex.

Contents

ILLUSTRATIONS
Photographs

Drawings

About the Author

James Tomlinson has been fishing from the age of four. He had his first angling article published in 1954 when he was fourteen and has contributed to all the leading British angling publications on fishing and casting over the past twenty years. He has fished for trout and salmon in many lochs, reservoirs and rivers in this country and abroad, he also runs angling courses on the world-famous River Tweed.

He was the All-round British Amateur Casting Champion and is now the current World All-round Professional Fly Casting Champion and has held eleven British Casting records, including fly accuracy, fly accuracy and distance, and trout and salmon distance using ordinary fishing tackle. He became Joint World-Record Holder by equalling the World fly Accuracy Record with one hundred points maximum at the World Championships in America in 1981. He has been competing at National, International and World level in Casting Tournaments for the past fourteen years and has represented Britain as Team Captain in several World Championships. The countries in which he has competed include, Sweden, Austria, USA, USSR, Belgium and Holland.

Jim is also Chairman of the British Casting Association and a Director of the International Casting Federation, the overall governing body of the sport of Casting. He is also a member of the Scottish Association of Angling Instructors and in 1977 was appointed by the Secretary of State for Scotland under the Freshwater and Salmon Fisheries (Scotland) Act 1976 to give advice on the angling waters in the Strathclyde Region. He is married and lives with his wife and two children in Prestwick, Ayrshire.

Dedication
TO MY LATE FATHER
WHO FIRST INTRODUCED ME TO FISHING

Acknowledgements

I wish to express my sincere thanks to Isobel Martin, Tourist Officer, Dumbarton District Council, and Jean Swan for typing the manuscript, also Clive Couch and Jim Roddy for taking the photographs. My sincere thanks also go to Dr Frank Johnstone, former Secretary of Ardrossan Eglinton Angling Club who gave me so much encouragement when I began fly fishing. I wish also to thank John Wilshaw, Editor of 'Trout Fisherman' for allowing me to use some of my photographs which have appeared in that magazine.

James Tomlinson

Introduction

Every year more fly fishers are turning to stillwaters for their sport and this trend will be greatly increased in future years as new reservoirs open up near centres of population. Many river anglers are finding that it is just as exciting fishing stillwaters as running waters and are following the stillwater trend. Obscure lochs, particularly in the Highlands and Islands of Scotland offer first-class fishing and many dyed-in-the-wool river fishers have found that by treating these lochs as large pools in a river they have had excellent sport. Who knows – fly fishers of the future may confine themselves only to this type of fishing.

I have been lucky to live in an area where there has been good stillwater and river fishing within a short travelling distance from my house. My preference, however, has always been for stillwater fishing and each outing is a new challenge to me. One of the reasons for this is that large water areas change so quickly that it may be necessary to use several different fly techniques in the course of a day or an evening's fishing to achieve results. It is this search for the right taking method which, to me, is one of the great attractions of a stillwater.

Reservoirs and lochs give great scope for experiment. It is not a game of 'chuck and chance' as was once thought and it is the thinking angler – the one who can make his tackle work effectively for him under different conditions and who presents his flies and lures properly, who gets the results. Freedom from worry about your casting ability means that you can channel your efforts into concentrating on catching fish. Many opportunities to catch fish are lost because the angler comes up against a situation where he has to over-concentrate on his casting ability and fly presentation because of high banks, vegetation or strong winds, and loses the chance of covering the fish. It is worth spending the time mastering the various fly-casting techniques which can be used in different situations in stillwaters. The casting techniques in this book are ones which I found helped me greatly in increasing my seasonal catches from stillwaters.

I have been fishing stillwaters for twenty-five years and, during the past ten, have put my knowledge, gleaned from competing in national and international casting tournaments, to effective use. Before 1970 (the year I began tournament casting) I relied mainly on the overhead cast for stillwater fishing. In this book I shall explain a variety of casting techniques, including roll, side, double-haul and various adaptations which I have found to be extremely effective in stillwater angling.

The ability to use a wide variety of casting forms proficiently gives the angler a great advantage – anxiety about whether or not you can cover a particular fish is not conducive to fish catching. Many anglers claim that competition casters *can* cast but *can't* fish – the only thing I can say on that score is that I have fished with many world-class casters in this country and abroad, and all have proved superb fishermen. A good example was when fishing with two very good friends from Belgium (Hugo Mortel and Guido Vinck) last summer when conditions were completely against us for stillwater fishing – flat calms and sunshine with trout rising well out, or in the shade, with a background of high vegetation where a back cast was impossible. Using the double-haul and roll-cast we secured fourteen trout between us. Guido, who was the world fly accuracy champion in 1978 and has several other gold medals to his credit, covered the water at an amazing rate and reached fish with pinpoint accuracy. I was using a shooting head to reach the slight ripple well over forty yards out and took trout in that area; Hugo picked up three nice trout by employing the roll-cast with his back to the trees.

I think it is appropriate to end this introduction with the motto of the casting Club of Amsterdam 'Better Casting – Better Fishing.'

Tackle for Stillwater Fly Fishing

When choosing tackle for stillwater fly fishing it is necessary to consider whether your preference is for bank or boat fishing. If it is bank fishing, further consider the style of fishing – orthodox wet fly, nymph fishing or long-range wet fly and lure fishing with a shooting head, and then choose the tackle which will be most effective for it. Much time and many fish are lost because the angler has not taken the time to select the correct tackle for a particular style of fishing.

Vast sums of money are spent every year by anglers on unsuitable tackle for stillwater fishing. Often they rush into a tackle shop and ask for a rod for reservoir fishing without first considering the water they will be fishing and the style of fishing which is most likely to give the best results. Too often many anglers read that a particular rod adds 25% to their casting distance and they buy such a rod only to find that this is not the case. It is the correct casting technique that gets the extra yards, not the buying of expensive rods. The glass blank I used to win the trout fly accuracy event in the Scottish Open Championship in 1977 cost only £5. Pounds can be saved by making your own rods. Select the blank you require with matching cork handle and then simply whip and varnish the rings. Many rod kits are available and a rod can be made up in an evening. I make nearly all my tournament rods and have saved pounds by doing this. It also gives more satisfaction when fish are caught, or events won, with rods of your own making.

How, then, do you go about selecting the blank or rod which will be most suitable for your type of stillwater fishing? First it is necessary to consider rod action, length and the line weight best suited to a particular action. There are basically three actions for a trout fly rod: (1) slow (or soft) action (2) mid action or (3) fast (or tip) action. Photographs 1-3 show the three types of rod in action.

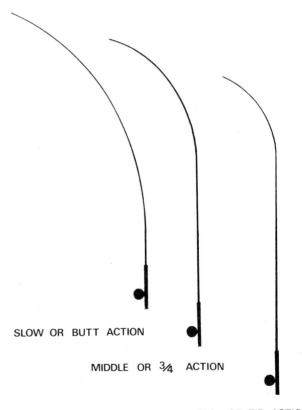

SLOW OR BUTT ACTION

MIDDLE OR ¾ ACTION

FAST OR TIP ACTION

Figure A shows a tip action rod and figure B a butt action rod. The shaded area is the part which flexes when the rod is in use. It can be seen that the shaded area in A is much smller than in B. The energy is concentrated towards the tip in A and provides a much quicker acceleration, which transmits the energy to the line and gives it the much greater speed which is essential for distance.

When the rod tip travels only a short distance a narrow arc is formed and hence a narrow line loop as in the above drawing. If the rod travels a long distance, a wide arc and wide line loop is formed. A narrow line loop is much better for accuracy and distance, since there is a smaller area to be affected by wind and air resistance.

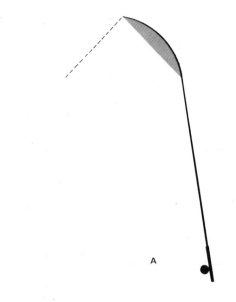

A

B

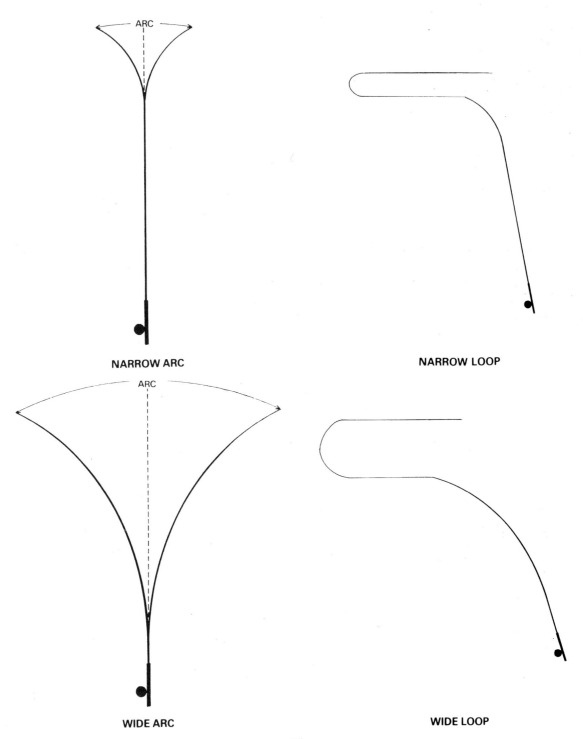

NARROW ARC

NARROW LOOP

WIDE ARC

WIDE LOOP

15

Slow action.

Medium action.

Photograph 1 shows a slow action; note that the casting curve is from the rod-tip right down to the casting hand. This type of action is best with light lines (AFTM 3 to 5) where distance is not required. If a heavy line is used it overloads the rod and kills its action. A long 10 or 11 ft soft-action rod is very good for boat fishing.

Photograph 2 shows mid or, as the Americans call it, a three-quarter action and this sums up the action of this type of rod. Note that the rod curve is from rod-tip to three-quarters down the rod. A medium-action rod is very good for orthodox wet fly and nymph fishing where often, because of the light leaders being used, a fairly light strike is required. This type of rod action is best used with medium AFTM 5-6 fly lines where average casting is required. You will find that the stiffer the rod becomes the heavier it feels; this is because the stiffer action presents more resistance to the casting muscles. However this casting 'feel' disappears as you get accustomed to a particular rod action.

Fast action.

Photograph 3 shows the action of a fast or tip-action rod. Note that most of the action is confined to the rod-tip. The middle section and butt are far less flexible than a slow or medium-action rod. A fast-action rod can impart greater tip-speed to the line and therefore the line can be cast faster and further. Fast-action rods are the best weapons for shooting heads and forward tapered lines for distance casting on reservoirs. A much tighter line loop can be cast when using this type of rod properly; therefore the fly can be presented much faster to the fish. A fast-action rod is the most effective for casting into the wind. It is essential to use the correct line weight with fast-action rods. Normally, lines and shooting heads AFTM 7, 8 or 9 are the most suitable for this action. Many anglers make the mistake of using too light a line which does not bring out the power of a fast rod. The use of the wrong line weight only results in tiring the caster.

Rod length is also very important. Many anglers believe that the longer a single-handed rod is the further they can cast. Apart from boat fishing where a long rod can be advantageous for working the fly on a short line, I do not go beyond 9ft 6in for a stillwater rod. Rods longer than this mean more weight in the hand and the extra length exerts more leverage against the caster, resulting in fatigue. Anything which tires the caster and affects casting and fly presentation in stillwater fishing should be eliminated. Long rods, heavy rods and reels, and wrong lines only result in a tired casting arm and affect the concentration of the caster which in turn affects the number of offers hooked.

Often one finds an angler fishing from the bank with a rod of between 10 and 11 ft and a heavy reel and, when asked about this, states that the heavy reel balances the rod. This is nonsense: a heavy reel is only more weight in the hand, which has to be moved every time you make a cast. Often one also sees a very light carbon rod weighing between $3\frac{1}{2}$ and 4 oz being used with a reel of between $6\frac{1}{2}$ and 8 oz – again more weight in the hand. So long as it is functional and has enough line capacity, the reel should be as light as possible.

As I have said, select the rod action (together with the correct line) which is going to be most appropriate to your type of fishing. If you are going to be involved in more than one type of stillwater fishing, e.g. boat fishing and distance work, then get two different actions of blank and make up two rods. If you don't want to make the rods yourself and you know a friend who has a rod which you feel will suit your type of fishing ask him to let you try it – it is always much better to try the rod in a fishing situation with rod, reel and line. You never get to know how the rod will perform simply by waving it about a few times in the tackle shop. Line load and water drag can make a tremendous difference to the 'feel', so try out the rod if at all possible by the waterside.

Photographs 1, 2 and 3 show the three rods I use for different styles of stillwater angling. Rods 1 and 2 are tip-action fibre-glass rods and most of my reservoir fishing is done with them. These rods are 9ft long and one has a 6in butt extension, which is very useful for keeping the reel away from the clothes when playing large fish and also for exerting more pressure. I have had these rods for over ten years and, apart from using them constantly in the reservoirs, since then I have won both the Scottish and British Skish (this is using ordinary fishing equipment) trout fly distance, and the furthest I have cast in a tournament on water with this equipment is 47 metres (52 yards). This was with a shooting head of 44ft 3in of No.8 sinking line. I often use this shooting head on stillwaters when the fish are really far out and have taken many fish well over 45 yards from the bank (I measured the amount of line I had out after the fish were caught). This shows the potential of ordinary rods and the distance at which trout can be hooked and landed.

The tip-action rod I use for distance work.

Tip-action rod. (Note the curve near the top of the rod when playing a fish.)

Medium-action rod.

The rod in Photograph 3 is the one I use for orthodox wet fly and nymph fishing. It has a mid-action and is very suitable for this type of fishing. I use fairly light monofilament of around $3\frac{1}{2}$lbs for nymph fishing and this softer action rod allows a gentler strike, which is necessary when fishing light. It has, however, sufficient backbone to cast the double tapered line I use for nymph fishing a fair distance. The rod I use for boat fishing is a light soft-action 10ft glass rod – not particularly good for any great distances but ideal for 'working' the bob fly on a short line. As for lines – as I said earlier it is the weight of fly line to be cast which determines the rod action which can best propel a particular weight. Many anglers forget that a flyline is basically an elongated weight. The AFTM line system is based on the weight of the first 30ft of line which, when aerialised, flexes the rod properly. The higher the line number, the heavier the line. However, rods can

handle different line weights and this is done by increasing or decreasing the line weight by lengthening or shortening the length of line in order to get the correct length which flexes the rod properly. A rod which has an AFTM 7 rating can be used with a No.6 line simply by having more line which will increase the weight in the air. Always think in terms of the flyline as an elongated weight and this should help you to understand the relationship between the line and the rod.

The handle of one of my distance rods showing the butt extension closed.

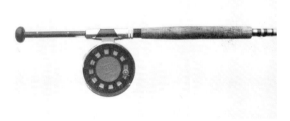

The butt extension open. (Note the butt extension in use in Photograph 1.)

The handles of my two distance rods.

Basically there are three types of line for stillwater fishing – (1) double taper (2) forward taper (3) shooting head. A fourth type, the level line, can be very useful for boat fishing. I used a very light No.1 Kingfisher silk level line with my soft boat rod for years and had excellent results with it. I now use a No.3 line with this rod.

Double-tapered lines are probably the most popular lines for orthodox wet fly and nymph fishing on reservoirs. The advantage of the double-tapered line is that it can be picked up quickly off the water, and this is of particular use when a quick change of direction is required. Double-tapered lines are easier to retrieve, particularly by the figure-of-eight technique. Another advantage of double-taper lines is that when one taper starts to wear it is just a matter of reversing the line on the reel and you virtually have a new line. It pays to buy a good double-tapered line – properly cared for it will give several years of use.

Forward-tapered lines are designed for distance casting. They are constructed with a heavy front section followed by a much thinner line which shoots easily. These lines are good for casting into the wind and for distance; also, compared with monofilament, the thin shooting line is fairly easily retrieved. These lines are costly and I prefer to make my own lines for distance work on reservoirs.

Shooting heads attached to monofilament are the lines to use for maximum distance. The 'heads' can be attached to other thin shooting lines e.g. braided nylon, dacron or thin backing line, which are all easier to handle than monofilament.

It is a good idea to buy some mill-end fly lines and make your own shooting heads, both floating and sinking. These mill-end lines are cheap and come in a variety of sizes and line weights from AFTM 6 to 9. Try lengths from 34 to 37ft to start with, using a fast-action 9ft rod. When you become more proficient in

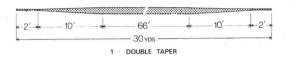

1 : DOUBLE TAPER

2 : WEIGHT FORWARD

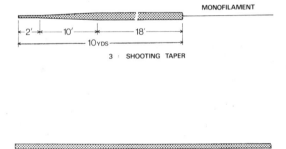

3 : SHOOTING TAPER

4 : LEVEL

handling a shooting head, you can increase the length. However, as I will explain in the section on the double haul, learn the proper distance casting technique with a double-tapering line before going on to long shooting heads. I use shooting heads of up to 44ft on reservoirs – more than this can lead to difficulties, particularly in bad conditions.

Once you have mastered distance casting it is up to you to find the shooting head which you feel you can handle with ease. There are several methods of attaching them to monofilament and other lines, but I find the following to be as good as any.

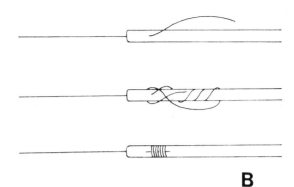

B

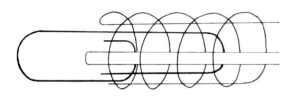

The second method is very popular and is known as the needle knot. The monofilament is threaded through the centre of the line for about $\frac{1}{4}$in. The needle is then passed through the line as shown. Pull about 4in of monofilament through the hole and whip finish.

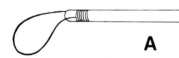

A

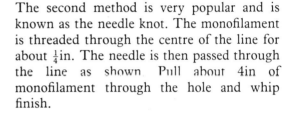

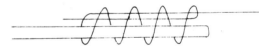

The first method is to take a 2in. length of braided nylon and pass this through the fly line with a needle as shown, whip finish and varnish the join. Leave for a few hours to set.

C

The advantage of having a loop at the end of the shooting head is that the head can be changed quickly. I always carry both floating and sinking shooting heads together with a double- tapered fly line when I go fishing. I am then prepared for ordinary wet fly and nymph fishing with the double-taper line, and long-range fishing to either rising fish or searching the water at distance with my floating and sinking shooting heads.

The knot I use is similar to the above but is all external. I use this knot for attaching tournament and stillwater shooting heads and it has never let me down. The knot can be made very quickly. Pass the monofilament four times over the end of the fly line as shown in the sketch and then insert the end of the monofilament through the formed loops and pull both ends of the mono tight. Varnish the join.

Thin line, particularly monofilament, when wound on the reel forms little loops which make shooting line very difficult. Try and find a light wide-diameter reel, particularly when using mono – this helps greatly in increasing the size of the line coils. It is also a good idea to stretch the monofilament before fishing – this helps to prevent the line kinking and forming coils. As I said earlier, it is often the simplest points in casting and choice of tackle which cause frustration. Something which often proves very troublesome to the caster is an unsuitable cork grip – too thick a grip strains the hand and one which is too thin gives poor rod control. It is a simple matter to sandpaper a fat grip to suit your hand and thin grips can easily be stripped and built up. Think about the matters which are giving you problems, and you will probably find that they can be very easily rectified.

A selection of fly reels.

A large diameter reel, ideal for monofilament.

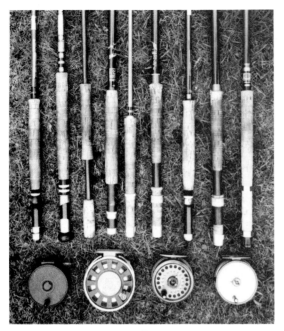

Various rod handles and fittings

A selection of glass and carbon reservoir rods. (Note the diameter difference.)

A fat and slim handle. (Note the difference in diameter between glass and carbon.)

Two tournament open trout fly distance rods. The furthest I have cast in a tournament with a 50ft shooting head is 66 yds, and, in practice, 74 yds.

23

I prefer Fuji rings throughout, with the butt ring being a two-legged Fuji and the intermediate rings single-legged. My experiments with various rod rings have convinced me that Fuji rings give more distance.

ROD RING TYPES

OFF SET BRIDGE RINGS

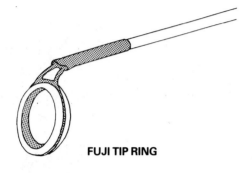

FUJI TIP RING

SNAKE RINGS

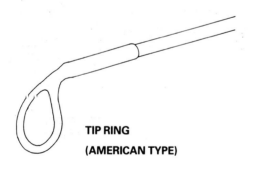

TIP RING
(AMERICAN TYPE)

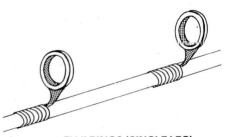

FUJI RINGS (SINGLE LEG)

Casting Fundamentals

Failing to grasp the fundamentals in the early stages of a skill leads to difficulties later on and, in particular, when trying to iron out ingrained bad habits. It is a great pity that a fraction of the time anglers spend on selecting equipment and reading tackle catalogues is not spent on improving their casting technique. A little time considering the mechanics of fly casting in the early stages of the skill, so that the various movements become effortless, cuts out much of the frustration in a fly fisher's angling life.

It is often the simplest points which present a great deal of trouble – an example being the wrong way of holding a rod. The rod grip is very important, particularly in stillwater fishing where long casting is often required. Before discussing the movements in single-handed fly casting let us look at and try out the ways of holding a rod. Photograph 1 shows the index finger extended along the handle, the grip often used by newcomers to stillwater fly fishing. Using this grip when casting on stillwaters results not only in straining the finger but also in restricting the back cast movement.

The thumb along the top of the handle in Photograph 2 is much better and often used, particularly for long back casts.

It is best, however, to use the grip shown in Photograph 3 with the thumb angled to the left; this is a much more relaxed grip and allows freer movement of the wrist.

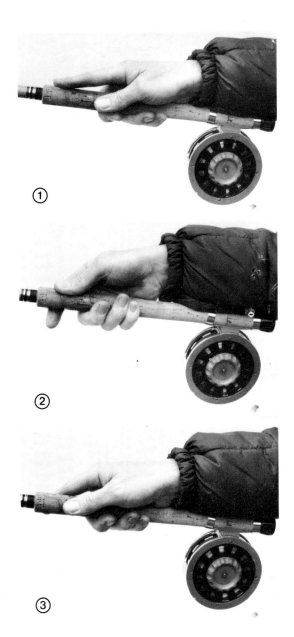

① ② ③

Once you are satisfied with your grip, put on the line, leader and reel and lay out some 40ft of line in front of you and hold the line as shown in Photograph 4. Get into the habit of keeping tension on the section of line between the butt ring and free hand in both back and forward casts. I shall return to this point a great deal throughout the book since it is of utmost importance in proper line control and line speed.

Before making any rod movement let us consider the position of feet and legs, for these play an important part, especially for long casting on stillwaters, so it is best to get this correct from the start. For a right-handed caster the feet should be angled to the right and be about 21 in apart for normal casting, but for longer casts, as will be explained in the section on the double haul, the stance is wider. Angling the feet to the right makes it easier to watch the line in the back cast, and the proper width of stance gives good body weight distribution. These simple points help considerably in establishing the basis for a sound casting technique.

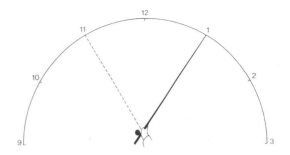

To understand the various casting arcs it helps to visualise a clock face. In normal casting the arc of rod movement is from eleven to one.

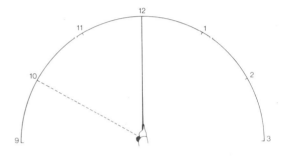

For a high back cast the arc should be tilted forward as shown in this diagram.

Shooting line: in order to achieve distance in the forward cast, strip a few yards of line from the reel and leave in loose coils at your feet. As the rod reaches the ten o'clock position in the forward cast, release line with the left hand and the loose coils will shoot out and extend the length of cast. Follow through to the horizontal as shown.

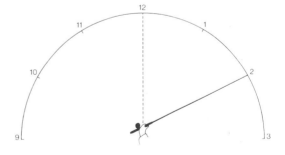

For a low back cast the arc should be tilted backward as shown here.

The next set of photographs show various stages in rod positioning for the forward and back cast of the ordinary trout fly cast, which will help to clarify the mechanics of the operation. The rod can be used through a wide or a narrow arc when performing the trout fly cast. Using the rod through a wide arc as shown in Photographs 1 and 2 results in the line forming a wide loop. This wide loop is a great handicap to distance casting on reservoirs as it offers a greater area for air and wind resistance. Accuracy, particularly in the wind, is also impaired because a wide line loop has poor line speed and is not nearly so positive in presenting the fly or lure.

Tapered balanced leaders are essential for good fly presentation, proper line turnover and casting into the wind. The butt section of the leader should be practically as thick as the end of the fly line tapering to the point. The size of the fly or lure is important in relation to the leader point. The larger the fly the heavier the point and vice versa. A large fly on a thin point will result in poor control and presentation on the forward cast. Leaders can be constructed by using various thicknesses of monofilament starting from 20 lb breaking strain at the end of the fly line to between 4 and 8 lb at the point of the leader. I prefer to have a permanent 2ft length of monofilament tied by a nail knot (as explained elsewhere in the book) to the end of the fly line. I attach my leaders by means of the simple blood knot to this 2ft length of monofilament. I also prefer to buy knotless tapered leaders. Most of my fly fishing on stillwaters is done with an 11ft leader on which I normally use three flies. However, for nymph and lure fishing I prefer a long 16ft leader.

For river fishing I use much shorter leaders which are also tapered. I find leaders of between 8ft and 5ft 6ins are best.

Using the rod through a wide arc.

Now look at Photographs 3-5, which shows the rod being used on a narrow arc which results in a narrow line loop – much better for distance casting, accuracy and line control. You will also note that the casting arm is moving backward and forward on the same plane. If the planes are separated (which is very common) and the angler starts making a circular motion, the line also follows this circular motion and consequently forms the undesirable wideline loop. Practise until you are casting with a good tight line loop.

Several angling writers in the past have advocated keeping the wrist stiff at the completion of the back cast. I must admit I used to cast with a stiff wrist before I got involved with tournament casting. Reading a great deal of physiology soon changed my opinion of this however and is worth explaining. Physiology has proved that the faster a muscle contracts the less force it is capable of exerting. In relation to casting the more we spread the accelerating forces of the whole arm the more force we are capable of exerting. This can be proved by locking the elbow and moving the upper arm. The hand will move at a given speed. If the elbow is then allowed to open and close the speed of the hand is increased without putting a greater load on the muscles which move the upper arm. Wrist movement will increase the speed of the hand further without increasing muscle load. This is very important since restricting the accelerating forces of the arm (including the wrist) leads to fatigue and affects casting form. It is the final flick of the wrist in the back and forward casts that imparts the greatest amount of tip speed to the line – locking the wrist prevents this. It would interest the reader to visit a British Casting Association tournament and observe that all the top casters break their wrist in the back cast and some very considerably. It is also interesting to note that none of the modern top casters at world and international casting tournaments use a stiff wrist.

The rod being used through a narrow arc.

Now try casting following this sequence: first, pillow the butt of the rod under the forearm (get into the habit of doing this – it gives much greater leverage for the start of the back cast which is particularly useful for long casting on stillwaters). The wrist should be turned down and the forearm at the horizontal at the start of the back cast. The forearm is moved vertically toward the head and then the wrist is flicked over at chin level and the movement stopped at just about eye level (Photographs 1-4). The 12 yards of line will end up on the ground behind you. Make sure it is straight since a straight back cast is the basis of a good forward cast.

You will see from Photographs 5-8 that the forward cast is the reverse of the back cast – flick the wrist over just before the rod reaches the horizontal and then allow the line to drift onto the ground. Always aim about four feet above the ground then follow through for good turnover and delicate presentation. If the cast is aimed too near the water instead of a few feet above, the splashy presentation often scares the fish.

The back cast: the wrist is flicked over at chin level.

The forward cast: flick the wrist over just before the rod reaches the horizontal.

Practise these movements, this time with the line in the air, remembering to keep the line between the butt ring and left hand tight in both back and forward casts, and not to separate the planes. Once you feel things are right, go through the same drill on the water. Never practise too long on land as this can lead to a lazy back cast due to there being no surface water tension at the start of the back cast.

When you feel you have mastered the back and forward casts, try varying the arc of rod movement to get a high back cast, which is very useful when there is a dam wall behind and also gives a low forward cast for casting into the wind. Stop the rod movement with the rod at about twelve o'clock.

Practise casting the high and low back casts until they can be done with ease. Understanding and applying the fundamentals of casting is necessary both for basic casting and for learning more advanced casting such as the double haul.

Low back cast.

High forward cast (useful when the wind is behind).

The high back cast is very useful when there is a high bank.

A very high back cast. (Note that the hand has been raised to increase the height of rod and line.)

For a low back cast, lower the rod on the back cast to two o'clock. This will rcsult in a high forward cast which is desirable for good distance when the wind is behind you.

Lowering the back cast when the wind is behind you also results in a tighter line loop and therefore helps to penetrate the wind. Always aim for a good straight back cast.

Common
Casting Faults

A very common fault amongst stillwater casters and one which is the most likely to scare fish is a splashy presentation in the forward delivery.

This is caused by keeping the power on too long in the forward cast through aiming the rod too low at the water; the result is that the line and leader land heavily, causing a considerable commotion on the water surface.

To cure this fault, imagine a level four feet above the water and try to cast along it, allowing the flies to *drift* on to the water. Soon you will get into the habit of aiming the rod at the correct height. Another technique for delicate fly presentation is to shoot a little line every time the line straightens out in the forward cast and you will find that the fly and leader land much more gently.

Another common reason for losing a good fish is the appearance of knots in the leader, thus weakening the material leading to a breakage. Knots appearing on the leader can be caused by (1) starting to forward cast before the line has had time to straighten in the back cast (this also results in flies being snapped off); (2) not lowering the power stroke enough when casting into the wind with the result that the leader doubles back on itself and often forms a knot. But probably the most common cause is tipping the rod forward first and then pushing forcibly with the casting hand. The rod should be pushed forward only at the end of the forward cast.

Snapping (or whip-cracking) the line in the back cast with the result that flies are often lost is very costly. It is caused by starting the forward cast too soon before the line has a chance to straighten in the back cast, or not putting sufficient effort into the back cast to ensure the line straightens out. A good forward cast can only be achieved if the back cast has been well executed and that means the line must be straight before the forward cast commences.

To correct these faults, watch the back cast and make sure the line straightens out before making the forward cast. Also ensure that sufficient power is put into the back cast to enable the line to straighten. Gradually, however, you will develop the correct 'feel' and know instinctively when the line straightens.

Pausing too long in the back cast or taking the rod too far back results in the line and flies catching up on the ground behind you. To avoid this, again get into the habit when learning of watching the line straighten in the back cast; when it straightens make the forward cast. Gradually you will be able to time the exact moment for making the forward cast and then it will be no longer necessary to watch the line at the rear.

When learning remember also not to let the rod drift beyond the one o'clock position, otherwise the line can also end up on the ground. Once your line control becomes more proficient by the correct use of the left hand however, you will be able to allow the rod to drift well back (particularly in the double haul technique) without the line touching the ground or water in the back cast.

False Casting

False casting is where the fly is cast but isn't allowed to touch the water. Carried out properly, false casting can be extremely useful to the stillwater angler. There are occasions when the dry fly can be very successful on reservoirs and it is then essential that the artificial be kept dry in order that it floats properly. To achieve this the fly is normally anointed with a silicone floatant and dried periodically with a piece of amadu.

However, when fish are rising hastily and being caught there is little time to carry out this procedure. False casting comes in handy in this situation, for by doing two or three false casts in the air the fly can be quickly dried and cast to the rising fish.

Another use for false casting is to change the direction of the cast without the line touching the water. Often when fishing a loch or reservoir, cruising trout are quickly sucking down flies from the surface. These large fish can change their direction quickly. If a fish is missed but is seen to be rising to flies in a different position, it is a simple matter to change direction by false casting.

A third application is to extend the line in the air before presenting the fly to a rising fish. Line is slipped out gradually with the left hand during false casting until the fish can be reached and, since the fly and line does not touch the water until the required moment, the chances of scaring the fish are greatly reduced.

The author has hauled the line in the back cast –
note the left hand moving towards the right hand,
and the position of the feet.

Distance Casting

It is wise when beginning to learn distance fly casting to tone up the casting muscles. This is particularly important after a long lay-off during the winter months. Casting muscles which are out of condition lead to a tired arm and result in a poor casting technique which exaggerates faults.

There are several ways in which to strengthen your casting muscles. The ones I prefer are the following: tie the end of a 3ft length of cord around a brick, next tie the other end of the cord onto the middle of a 2ft length of broom handle. Hold the broom handle at arm's length with the hands at shoulder width apart and rotate the handle towards you; when the brick reaches the handle, rotate in the opposite direction. Doing this for a few minutes every day will greatly strengthen your wrists and forearms in a comparatively short time. Another method is to fill a lemonade bottle with sand or earth, extend the arm sideways, and rotate the bottle with wrist only. These exercises, done for only five minutes a day for one week, tone up the casting arm remarkably well.

The double-haul technique can be learned with several rod actions and line weights. I found that it is worth practising for a time with a tip-action rod and No. 7 double-tapered line and then moving on fairly quickly to a shooting head of 34ft attached to 20 lbs breaking-strain monofilament.

When attempting to learn the double-haul, always get into the habit of keeping the line tight with the left hand and pulling the line down a few inches at the start of every back cast; this increases the line speed and gives greater control of the back cast. Remember also, when doing the forward cast, not only to keep tension on the line with the left hand to increase line speed but also to give another slight pull on the line. Getting into the habit of making these two small pulls helps greatly in understanding the 'feel' of the double-haul.

Anglers often run into difficulty because they are not taking time to master each part of the technique. Spending a little more time in practice until the whole operation can be done smoothly and efficiently is better than wasting a whole season thrashing about on the water simply because the technique was not properly mastered. It is much better to go through the various stages of the double-haul on land until the movements are mastered and then try the technique in water.

The first step is to run off 16 yds of line in front of you and then pull back 5 yds and drop it at your feet, which should be positioned as shown in Photograph 1. For a right-handed caster, the left foot is straight in front and the right foot angled to the right. This fairly wide stance helps greatly in distributing the forces. Using your legs properly is very important in the distance cast – a wide base not only allows stability but also means that a greater range of movement is possible. In all throwing actions whether javelin, discus or casting, the best results are achieved by applying the greatest amount of force over the greatest distance at the highest possible speed.

You should hold the rod firmly but not too tightly – a tight grip strains the hand and affects casting. I prefer my thumb to be at the side of the handle and not on top. Many anglers prefer to have their thumb on top of the handle for distance casting, but I find this restricts flexibility of the wrist; the handle should be pillowed under the forearm at the start of the back cast to allow more leverage.

Now to the back cast; with the left hand holding the line near the top of the rod handle, start to make an orthodox casting movement with your right hand, at the same time making a long haul (see Photograph 2) with the left hand. Ideally, the timing of the first haul should coincide with the fastest movement of the rod. This precise timing will come with practice. When you start the haul, turn your head and watch the line movement.

If you look at the photograph you will see that when the cast starts, the body weight is over the left leg and, as the movement progresses to the rear, the body weight is transferred onto the right leg. The line, because it has

The back and forward casts in the single-handed distance fly cast.

been hauled, is moving back a lot faster than in normal casting.

As the line loop is turning over in the back cast you will feel the line which is being held in the left hand being pulled upwards (see Photographs 3 and 4). Don't resist this – allow the left hand to move upwards towards the right (Photographs 5 and 6). You must always remember to maintain tension on the section of line between the left hand and the butt ring. You will also note that the body weight has been transferred to the right leg. Note in Photographs 6 and 7 how the tension is being kept on the line with the left hand. Note that the left hand holding the line has moved almost to the reel. From this position

This cast was performed in a strong following wind – the measured cast was just under 68 yds.

the forward cast begins.

Practice these movements until you have proper control of the line and remember to keep the line under tension throughout.

Several difficulties can arise at this stage of the technique and I would like to show how these can be overcome. The first haul during the back cast normally presents three main difficulties. The first, and most common one, is that, after hauling the line with the left hand, many anglers seem to forget about it and hold the line stationary down the left side of the body instead of allowing the left hand to move up towards the butt ring as the line is turning over. The left hand holding the line tight must start to move towards the butt ring as the main line begins to turn over during the back cast. When I was learning the technique and this problem arose, I made a shorter haul with my left hand which resulted in a much easier follow up to the butt ring with the left hand. Gradually as better control is obtained the haul can be lengthened.

The second common fault is the exact opposite of the first. The left hand is moved up too quickly after the haul is made during the back cast so that instead of waiting until the main portion of line outside the rod tip transmits its tension to the left hand, the angler allows the section of line between his holding hand and butt ring to go slack. The technique has now broken down before it has started since line speed and line control have been lost. Getting into the habit of watching the line as it is turning over in its back cast assists in the co-ordination of the left hand movement.

The third fault is holding the right hand too high at the completion of the back cast instead of keeping the hand low. Holding the line high on the back cast often results in the line being forced down to the ground too early in the forward cast. For good distance, the rod should start fairly low in the back cast and finish high in the forward cast. To overcome the high hand at the end of the back cast, get into the habit of bending the right leg and putting the body weight on this leg at the completion of the back cast, this will result in lowering the back and right arm. Partial straightening of the right arm to accommodate rod drift helps also. Once the movement starts to feel correct, practice for short periods only and then have a rest, for it is surprising how easy it is, particularly in the early stages, to pick up a fault when the arm gets tired and this fault becomes exaggerated with continued practice. If you feel a fault has crept in, stop and analyse your movements, then go back to the correct casting form.

Photographs 16 and 17 shows a long haul down the left side of the body; it is at this stage that difficulty often arises in following up with the left hand. If the haul is made shorter it is easier to control the line. Note also in these two photographs that the head has been turned and the line turn over can be easily followed – this assists greatly in helping to eradicate the second fault of the left hand following the line too quickly.

When comparing Photographs 2 and 4 you will note that the casting hand has dropped considerably. This has been achieved by transferring the body weight onto a bent right leg and by partially straightening the right arm.

Two rear-view shots in the distance cast: note the long haul at the start of the back cast and how near the left hand is to the reel at the end of the back cast.

Photographs 18-20 show the first haul of the technique on water. The rod is fairly far back so it is essential not to lose line speed in the back cast otherwise the main portion of line will only end up in the water behind you. Keep practising, but remember, as soon as a fault creeps in which interrupts the smoothness and continuity of the back cast, stop and try to rectify it as quickly as possible.

The second part of the double-haul is the line pull in the forward cast. This second line pull is vital for distance.

The simplest way to learn the forward cast is to allow the line to fall on to the ground at the completion of the back cast and then practice from that position. Make sure that the line is straight out on the ground behind you – a good straight back cast is the foundation of a good forward cast.

Photograph 8 shows that the casting arm is fairly low and the left hand holding the line is practically up to the reel. From this position start moving both hands forward at the same time. This is a very important point – many anglers at this stage make the mistake of moving one hand much faster than the other and the technique breaks down, so make sure that both hands are kept together and tension is kept on the line with the left hand.

At the start of the forward cast the body weight will be on the right leg, but as the forward cast progresses the body weight will move onto the left leg. Also, as the forward cast progresses, the hips pivot from the right to a square-on position (see Photographs 10 and 11). You will also see from these photographs that the casting arm is starting to move upward and the wrist is well open – this is important because it is the final flick of the wrist nearing completion of the forward cast that helps to impart the high speed to the rod tip essential for distance.

In Photograph 12 you will see that the left hand is about to haul the line. Full power

The fishing situation – high line speed must be maintained throughout.

should be applied just in front of the face. You will also see from this photograph that most of the body weight is on the left leg. These last few body movements will seem fairly slow to begin with but keep concentrating on the correct format and then speed up the movement. At the start of the forward cast, make use of the leg muscles – push off with the bent right leg, quickly pivot the hips to the front and (very important) keep the two hands coming through together.

In Photographs 13 and 14 the line has been hauled down the left side of the body. The wrist has also been turned over very quickly at this point. Notice how the left leg has straightened and acted as a brake to the left side.

Photograph 15 shows the follow through with the rod being lowered in order to minimise the friction of the line through the rings – holding the rod tip too high causes a wide angle between rod tip and line, causing a lot more friction and cutting down distance.

The pull in the forward cast, like the pull in the back cast, should coincide with the fastest rod movement, since a pull at the moment of fastest possible tip speed gives the greatest degree of energy to the line. A feeling for the precise moment will come with practice. Often, when practising the forward cast, you hit one just right and away goes the line like a bullet taking all the shooting line. So you take off more line, put it on the ground, and expect the next cast to go even further but it does not happen – probably because you are trying too hard and the correct form has broken down. It is best to stop when this happens, take a rest, and try again. Soon you will find you are getting several long casts in your practice sessions as your confidence builds up.

Once you feel you have mastered both forward and back casts by taking the line from the ground, try the technique with the line completely aerialised. Remember to concentrate on a good back cast, making sure that the line is straight out behind you before starting the forward cast – at all times keeping tension on the line with the left hand.

I found that it paid to spend some time learning distance casting with a double-tapered line, then move on to monofilament and a short shooting head of around 34ft Practice on land until you have the movements mastered before going onto water. Once you are satisfied with your technique you can experiment with longer shooting heads. It also pays to become acquainted with the various weather conditions as different wind speeds require variations in the casting arc for the best results.

The Side Cast

You'll often find, when fishing stillwaters, that the side cast is very useful, particularly when boat fishing when it helps to keep the rod away from your companion. It is also very useful when fishing in windy conditions, particularly casting along the wind.

To perform the side cast the rod is simply moved from the vertical position to the horizontal position. Practice from this position with only about 6 or 7 yds of line until you have proper control. Soon it will be found that the line can·be lengthened and controlled easily.

It is not possible to cast as far with the side cast as the overhead cast since the line is moving only two or three feet above the water. It is easy, however, to reach normal fishing distances once the side cast has been mastered. The timing is just the same as in the overhead cast.

When fishing the side cast on reservoirs where there is vegetation, it is a good idea to get into the habit of watching the back cast. By doing this the back cast can more easily be controlled and can be flicked through gaps in the vegetation to obtain a straight line before making the forward cast.

On the forward cast always remember to shoot a little line at the completion of the cast. This gives a much more delicate fly presentation.

The Roll and Switch Casts

There are places in lochs and reservoirs where, because of high dam walls, banking, vegetation or rock formations, it is very difficult (sometimes impossible) to use the overhead single fly cast, since the line cannot be cast to the rear. In these instances it is a great asset to be able to use the roll cast in which the line does not travel behind you. The roll cast must be practised on water and not on grass. The water drag is necessary to create tension in the line, which helps the line loop turn over.

The first step is to get sufficient line out in order to start the roll cast. This is done by holding the rod butt higher than the rod tip, then by an underhand action – flick the rod backwards and forwards at the same time slipping line out with the free hand until some 6 or 7 yds of line is in front of you.

The next step is to raise the rod slowly until it is just past twelve o'clock and make a smart downward stroke to ten o'clock. The rod should be stopped dead at this point. The line will now roll out in front of you and straighten. The rod should then be brought down to the horizontal position.

To speed up the roll cast and achieve a better fly presentation, hold the section of line between the butt ring and free hand – this will give much greater line speed and control. Shooting line should be done at the completion of power at ten o'clock.

The back view of the roll cast.

The switch cast.

46

The switch cast is a variation of the roll cast and is useful when there is vegetation both above and behind you. The line is extended as previously described in the roll cast but, instead of the rod being held in a vertical position, it is held in a horizontal position and the line quickly flicked down in the forward power stroke.

The roll cast.

Casting in
Windy Conditions

Although many anglers find strong wind a great hindrance, there is no reason not to use techniques which make the wind work *for* you.

When there is a strong wind behind you, it is necessary to put more power into the back cast to ensure that the line straightens. If the line does not straighten, the flies will often be snapped off when the forward cast is made. Once the line has straightened, the rod should be allowed to drift back to the two o'clock position instead of just after twelve o'clock. Taking the rod further past the vertical will lower the back cast and, when making the forward cast, the line will go out higher. This will make it catch the wind more easily and longer casts with less effort will be possible.

For casting *into* the wind the converse applies. The strong wind coming toward you will help to straighten the line in the back cast and the rod should be stopped just before twelve o'clock. This will cause the line to fly high on the back cast and on the forward cast it will be low, which is ideal for penetrating the wind. Remember to aim only about one foot above the water when casting into the wind, and to hold the section of line between the butt ring and the left hand tight. This allows for much greater line control and speed and results in a much tighter line loop, which is essential for casting into the wind. Photographs 1-5 show the technique for casting when there is a strong wind behind and Photographs 6-8 when casting into the wind.

Here I am using a very high line speed to prevent bank hook-up. It is better to move up the bank in a very strong wind.

Casting a long line with a strong following wind.
(Note the low back cast and high forward cast.)

The line being driven into the wind on the back
cast.

Casting into the wind.
(Note the high back cast and tension being maintained on the line with the left hand.)

The line is being punched into the wind. (Note
the low forward cast.)

Casting to Cruising Trout

Often the largest trout in stillwaters are cruisers, and efficient casting is necessry to hook them. Cruising trout can often present a problem in that they are moving fairly quickly, sucking down flies from the water surface or just under the surface film. It is necessary, therefore, to present the fly quickly in the path of the fish. The direction of the fish can be determined by watching the rings on the water surface caused by the feeding fish.

The object is to cast about $4\frac{1}{2}$ft in front of the last ring. This is achieved by condensing the casting movement: use a very narrow casting arc, applying power in a straight line between eleven o'clock and twelve o'clock, and follow through so that the line travels faster. Note the condensed rod movement in photographs 1 and 2.

A condensed rod movement for fast casting. (Line tension must be kept with the left hand.)

The rod is kept in the same plane for really accurate casting.

④ ⑤ ⑥

Cruising trout sometimes stop and feed in the same spot. It is in this situation that really accurate casting pays off on stillwater. For really accurate trout fly casting there should be no hurried movements of arm, rod or line – this interrupts correct casting form and affects the timing. The rod in the back and forward cast should move in the same plane. The angle of the plane is of little importance, it is the consistency of the plane which matters. If the planes of the rod are the same the fly line will follow a similar path and travel in a straight line, under control and presented accurately. The arm and rod should not stray far from the angler's side in accuracy casting – if they do there is more chance of making exaggerated inaccurate movements. Photographs 3-6 show the casting stroke for accurate casting in stillwaters.

Many anglers make the mistake when casting of moving the hand and rod in a semi-circular movement – they start the back cast with the arm angled well out from the body and continue this way until the completion of the back cast. Then, in the forward cast, they bring the arm in close to the body which results in the line following a similar route. Line speed is lost since the loop, which is now wider, is affected by air resistance and the fly presentation is poor. For really accurate casting on stillwaters it is essential not to separate the rod planes.

Casting in Rivers, Streams and Burns

Although this book is primarily about flycasting on stillwaters, the techniques described can be used equally well on rivers, streams and burns. I found that proficient roll and side casting, good fly presentation, accuracy and ability to cast into downstream wind are the most important aspects to concentrate on for success in running waters.

The points made in the section on choice of tackle for stillwaters apply also when selecting equipment for rivers and streams. Consider first the type of waters you intend fishing – large rivers, small rivers, streams or burns. Next, consider the fishing method you intend using most often – dry fly, wet fly and nymph or lure fishing. For fishing dry fly in large rivers I prefer a tip-action rod between 8ft 6in and 9ft capable of taking No.7 and 8 lines. This rod is very suitable for casting into a downstream wind, which is often necessary to reach good trout-holding spots when fishing the dry fly at the start of the season. This rod can also be used for single-handed salmon fishing.

My choice of rod for wet fly and nymph fishing would be one with a three-quarter action which allows for a slower and more gentle strike which is necessary when fishing across and downstream. In sea-trout fishing, too harsh a strike with a fast tip-action rod can tear the hook from the sea trout's soft mouth.

If your intention is to fish a lot of small streams and burns it is wise to invest in a short rod of 7ft 6in capable of taking a light, No.5, line. It is often not possible to cast more than a few yards in many burns because of trees and heavy bank vegetation and this is where efficient roll, switch, and side casting pay off. I prefer double-tapered lines for rivers, streams and burns and very rarely use forward tapered lines or shooting heads. Double tapered lines give much better presentation and are essential for efficient roll and switch casting. A short 5 or 6ft leader is much easier to control, particularly when fishing small waters, and gives a better line and fly turn over. Remember to use as light a rod and reel as possible – excess weight in the hand, particularly when there is a lot of false casting to be done, is tiring and impairs your technique.

A wet fly cast across the water – always shoot a little line at the completion of the cast for good presentation.

A long cast on a large river into headwind when
fishing the dry fly. (Note the low power stroke in
the forward cast.)

Roll casting on a small stream – always remember to make a powerful movement from twelve o'clock to ten o'clock and stop dead at this point. (Note the powerful stroke in picture 2.)

A switch cast.

A side cast when fishing streams with plenty of vegetation.

Remember always to look behind when side casting because it may be necessary to flick the back cast through a gap in the trees in order to get a straight line before making a forward cast. (Note that the rod is kept parallel to the river.)

Index